A LONG
OBEDIENCE
JOURNAL

EUGENE H. PETERSON
with Ruth Goring

InterVarsity Press
Downers Grove, Illinois

InterVarsity Press
P.O. Box 1400, Downers Grove, IL 60515
World Wide Web: www.ivpress.com
E-mail: mail@ivpress.com

InterVarsity Press® is the book-publishing division of InterVarsity Christian Fellowship/USA®, a student movement active on campus at hundreds of universities, colleges and schools of nursing in the United States of America, and a member movement of the International Fellowship of Evangelical Students. For information about local and regional activities, write Public Relations Dept., InterVarsity Christian Fellowship/USA, 6400 Schroeder Rd., P.O. Box 7895, Madison, WI 53707-7895.

All Scripture quotations, unless otherwise indicated, are taken from The Message *by Eugene H. Peterson. Used by permission of NavPress. All rights reserved.*

Cover photograph: Monica Dalmasso/Stone

Icons: Roberta Polfus

ISBN 0-8308-2039-6

Printed in the United States of America ∞

19	18	17	16	15	14	13	12	11	10	9	8	7	6	5	4	3	2	1
15	14	13	12	11	10	09	08	07	06	05	04	03	02	01	00			

Contents

Getting the Most out of the *Long Obedience Journal*

Our life day to day is a pilgrimage. We are traveling toward God. We are not merely trying to survive, or even simply to do the best we can. That is what it means to be Christian, to be human.

The Songs of Ascents (Ps 120—134), sung by the ancient Israelites as they trekked from their farms and villages to the great feasts in Jerusalem—the Feast of Passover, the Feast of Pentecost and the Feast of Tabernacles—are pilgrim songs. Their word-pictures make vivid for us what it means to be a pilgrim, to undertake an intentional journey into God's goodness and truth. As we meditate on them, they inform our steps, remind us of God's mercy, encourage us to persevere.

This journal, a companion to *A Long Obedience in the Same Direction,* is intended to enrich your encounter with the Songs of Ascents and draw you into a deeper life with God. Because paradoxically, we travel *toward* God yet find God already *with us*—Immanuel, walking with us, making himself known, suffering with us, forgiving and transforming us, giving us good gifts.

Roam through the journal and let it serve you. Its chapters parallel those of *A Long Obedience,* and each includes complete text of the relevant psalm, divided into sections so you can savor it slowly. The journal's questions and exercises will help you open your life to the Songs of Ascents. With some variation in order and space, chapters include the following elements.

Beginning to Obey ────────────────
Examine your life in light of our culture and consider how God may be calling you.

Pondering the Word ────────────────
Look closely at one or more passages of Scripture.

Recording Your Journey ──────────
Consider how God has guided and protected you thus far.

Writing to God ────────────────────
Respond to God directly through meditation, thanksgiving, supplication and listening prayer.

Worshiping God ───────────────────
Revel in God's generosity and faithfulness.

Jesus told his follower Thomas, "I am the Road, also the Truth, also the Life. No one gets to the Father apart from me" (Jn 14:5-6). A little later he promised, "I will not leave you orphaned; I am coming to you. . . . Those who love me will keep my word, and my Father will love them, and we will come to them and make our home with them" (Jn 14:18, 23 NRSV). The journey has an end: we come home to the life of God, and the eternal God makes his home in us.

One

DISCIPLESHIP

"What Makes You Think You Can Race Against Horses?"

Beginning to Obey ———————————

Being a *disciple* means we are people who spend our lives apprenticed to our master, Jesus Christ. We are in a growing-learning relationship, always. The word *pilgrim* tells us we are people who spend our lives going someplace, going to God, and whose path for getting there is the way, Jesus Christ.

What "skills in faith" is God calling you to develop as you follow Jesus?

What are the differences between a tourist and a pilgrim?

In your journey toward God, where do you need to stop being a tourist and learn to be a pilgrim?

Writing to God ─────────────────────────

"And [Moses] said to [God,] 'If your presence will not go, do not carry us up from here. For how shall it be known that I have found favor in your sight, I and your people, unless you go with us?'" (Ex 33:34-35 NRSV). Write a prayer inviting God's presence as you enter the journey of this journal.

Recording Your Journey ——————————————
We assume that if something can be done at all, it can be done quickly and efficiently. There is a great market for religious experience in our world; there is little enthusiasm for the patient acquisition of virtue, little inclination to sign up for a long apprenticeship in what earlier generations of Christians called holiness.

God does sometimes bring about rapid transformation in people's lives. Describe a time when you underwent fairly effortless and speedy change.

Have there been areas in which growth and transformation have come slowly?

Write an account of one change that God has been working into your life over a period of years.

Thomas Szasz, in his therapy and writing, has attempted to revive respect for what he calls the "simplest and most ancient of human truths: namely, that life is an arduous and tragic struggle; that what we call 'sanity,' what we mean by 'not being schizophrenic,' has a great deal to do with competence, earned by struggling for excellence; with compassion, hard won by confronting conflict; and with modesty and patience, acquired through silence and suffering."

Choose one of the cause-and-effect developments Szasz lists and write about how it has played out in the life of someone you admire.

struggling for excellence ⟶ competence
confronting conflict ⟶ compassion
silence and suffering ⟶ modesty and patience

Pondering the Word
In Romans 5:3-5 the apostle Paul describes a cause-and-effect movement similar to Szasz's:

We continue to shout our praise even when we're hemmed in with troubles, because we know how troubles can develop passionate patience in us, and how that patience in turn forges the tempered steel of virtue, keeping us alert for whatever God will do next. In alert expectancy such as this, we're never left feeling shortchanged. Quite the contrary—we can't round up enough containers to hold everything God generously pours into our lives through the Holy Spirit!

Meditate on the "developmental map" Paul delineates. Where would you place yourself on it and why?

hemmed in with troubles
        passionate patience
                tempered steel of virtue
                        alert expectancy

"We can't round up enough containers to hold everything God generously pours into our lives."

Make a list of the good gifts God has poured into your life "through the Holy Spirit." If you have trouble filling the page, continue with a prayer asking God to sharpen your awareness of his generous blessings.

Worshiping God

You will sing! sing through an all-night holy feast; your
hearts will burst with song, make music like the sounds
of flutes on parade, en route to the mountain of God, on their
way to the Rock of Israel. (Is 30:29)

Paul Goodman beseeched God, "Teach me a travel song." Pray
your thanks for God's help thus far in your journey.

Two

REPENTANCE

"I'm Doomed to Live in Meshech"
Psalm 120

 Pondering the Word ————————————

I'm in trouble. I cry to GOD,
    desperate for an answer.
"Deliver me from the liars, GOD!
    They smile so sweetly but lie through their teeth."

Have you, or has someone you know, ever felt frustrated and helpless because someone's well-camouflaged lies were causing serious harm?

How does the psalmist's cry—desperate though it is—show confidence in God's character?

Jesus says, "I am the Road, also the Truth, also the Life" (Jn 14:6). What does it mean that Jesus is Truth?

Beginning to Obey ────────────────

A person has to get fed up with the ways of the world before he, before she, acquires an appetite for the world of grace. We have been told the lie ever since we can remember: that human beings are basically nice and good. Everyone is born equal and innocent and self-sufficient. The world is a pleasant, harmless place. We are born free. If we are in chains now, it is someone's fault, and we can correct it with just a little more intelligence or effort or time. Christian consciousness begins in the painful realization that what we had assumed was the truth is in fact a lie.

What are some statements (from family, school, workplace or popular culture) that you once accepted as true but later learned are lies?

Such lies take root in us and lead us away from God, away from abundant life. Give an example—from your own life or someone else's—of one lie's destructive effects.

How is God calling you to stand against the lies?

Recording Your Journey ————————————
The first step toward God is a step away from the
lies of the world. The usual biblical word describing
the no we say to the world's lies and the yes we say to God's
truth is *repentance*. Repentance is a decision. It is deciding that
you have been wrong in supposing that you could manage your
own life and be your own god. It is a decision to follow Jesus
Christ and become his pilgrim in the path of peace.

Repentance means turning or changing direction. When in the
past have you entered into a repentance—a long-term change
undertaken with God's help?

What did you give up or turn away from?

What were the effects?

Do you know what's next, can you see what's coming,
    all you barefaced liars?
Pointed arrows and burning coals
    will be your reward.

Whenever we say no to one way of life that we have long been used to, there is pain. But when the way of life is in fact a way of death, a way of war, the quicker we leave it the better. Any hurt is worth it that puts us on the path of peace, setting us free for the pursuit, in Christ, of eternal life.

Describe a time when pain of some kind ("pointed arrows and burning coals") brought you to a point of healthy dissatisfaction with your life's status quo.

Tell of a time (perhaps immediately following the one above) when repentance required a painful renunciation.

Writing to God

In all immigrant stories there are mixed parts of escape and adventure: the escape from an unpleasant situation, the adventure of a far better way of life, free for new things, open for growth and creativity. Every Christian has some variation on this immigrant plot to tell.

Where is your "immigrant story" leading you now? For example, is God calling you to take a new step of repentance?

Spend at least fifteen minutes in silence, inviting the Spirit to speak to you. Confess any lies that have held sway in your life. Write down any commitments you decide to make, any Scriptures that come to mind and any words God seems to be speaking to you.

I'm doomed to live in Meshech,
  cursed with a home in Kedar.
My whole life lived camping
  among quarreling neighbors.
I'm all for peace, but the minute
  I tell them so, they go to war!

Worshiping God

Repentance, the first word in Christian immigration, sets us on the way to traveling in the light. It is a rejection that is also an acceptance, a leaving that develops into an arriving, a no to the world that is a yes to God.

God wants you to live in the light. Write your thanks for his lavish care, for his unwillingness to leave you trapped in lies.

Three

PROVIDENCE

"GOD Guards You from Every Evil"
Psalm 121

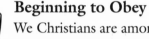 **Beginning to Obey** ——————————

We Christians are among that privileged company of persons who don't have accidents, who don't have arguments with our spouses, who aren't misunderstood by our peers, whose children do not disobey us. If any of those things should happen, it is a sign that something is wrong with our relationship with God.

Is that what you believe? If it is, I have some incredibly good news for you. You are wrong.

Where have you heard the "good Christians are always happy and healthy" message?

Why do you think this misguided belief is especially popular among North American Christians (as opposed to Christians in other parts of the world)?

Pondering the Word

I look up to the mountains;
  does my strength come from mountains?
No, my strength comes from GOD,
  who made heaven, and earth, and mountains.
He won't let you stumble,
  your Guardian God won't fall asleep.
Not on your life! Israel's
  Guardian will never doze or sleep.

The Creator is always awake: he will never doze or sleep. The Creator is Lord over time: he "guards you when you leave and when you return," your beginnings and your endings. The Creator is Lord over all natural and supernatural forces: he made them.

In Psalm 121 eight times God is described as the *guardian,* or as the one who guards. Do you think the way to tell the story of the Christian journey is to describe its trials and tribulations? It is not. It is to name and to describe God who preserves, accompanies and rules us.

Meditate on the truths about God that Psalm 121 celebrates. Think of ways God has revealed these aspects of his nature in Scripture, your own life, the lives of others.

GOD's your Guardian,
    right at your side to protect you—
Shielding you from sunstroke,
    shielding you from moonstroke.
GOD guards you from every evil,
    he guards your very life.

All the water in all the oceans cannot sink a ship unless it gets inside. Nor can all the trouble in the world harm us unless it gets within us. None of the things that happen to you, none of the troubles you encounter, have any power to get between you and God, dilute his grace in you, divert his will from you (see Rom 8:28, 31-32).

Read Romans 8:28-39. According to verses 28-30, what are God's purposes for you?

What evidence does verse 28 give of God's determination to take care of us?

How can we distinguish satanic condemnation from the Spirit's conviction of sin?

How can verses 33-34 help you face down the Accuser?

Read the passage aloud, inserting your own name wherever appropriate. ("We know that all things work together for good for Ruth, who loves God . . .")

Recording Your Journey ─────────────

The great danger of Christian discipleship is that we should have two religions: a glorious, biblical Sunday gospel that sets us free from the world, that in the cross and resurrection of Christ makes eternity alive in us, a magnificent gospel of Genesis and Romans and Revelation; and, then, an everyday religion that we make do with during the week between the time of leaving the world and arriving in heaven. We know that God created the universe and has accomplished our eternal salvation. But we can't believe that he condescends to watch the soap opera of our daily trials and tribulations; so we purchase our own remedies for that. To ask him to deal with what troubles us each day is like asking a famous surgeon to put iodine on a scratch.

Where do you find discrepancies between your Sunday experience of God and the way you relate to God day to day?

Do you know someone who has learned to bring daily trials to God? What can you learn from their example?

Writing to God ————————————————

The God of Genesis 1 who brought light out of darkness is also the God of this day who guards you from every evil.

Take time to bring God "the soap opera of your daily trials and tribulations"—struggles you face at work, in your family, with finances, in relationships with friends, neighbors or church leaders. Where do you especially need to be guarded from evil?

Worshiping God

He guards you when you leave and when you
   return,
   he guards you now, he guards you always.

Life is created and shaped by God, and the life of faith is a daily exploration of the constant and countless ways in which God's grace and love are experienced. Faith is not a precarious affair of chance escape from satanic assaults. It is the solid, massive, secure experience of God, who keeps all evil from getting inside us, who guards our life, who guards us when we leave and when we return, who guards us now, who guards us always.

Thank God for a few of the "constant and countless ways" you have experienced his grace, protection and love.

Four

WORSHIP

"Let's Go to the House of GOD"
Psalm 122

 Beginning to Obey ─────────────

When they said, "Let's go to the house of GOD,"
    my heart leaped for joy.
And now we're here, oh Jerusalem,
    inside Jerusalem's walls!
Jerusalem, well-built city,
    built as a place for worship!
The city to which the tribes ascend,
    all GOD's tribes go up to worship.

Why do we worship? Because worship gives us a workable structure for life. In worship all the scattered fragments of experience, all the bits and pieces of truth and feeling and perception are put together in a single whole. Outer quarrels and misunderstandings and differences pale into insignificance as the inner unity of what God builds in the act of worship is demonstrated. In worship we get a working definition for life: the way God created us, the ways he leads us. We know where we stand.

Consider the various elements of corporate worship listed on page 31 and how they come together to build a unified framework for your life.

praise

Scripture reading

confession

teaching/sermon

creed

fellowship

prayer

Lord's Supper/Eucharist

blessing

Recording Your Journey
To give thanks to the name of GOD—
this is what it means to be Israel.

Worship nurtures our need to be in relationship with God. "A Christian," wrote Augustine, "should be an alleluia from head to foot." But we do not worship because we *feel* like it. The wisdom of God says that we can *act* ourselves into a new way of feeling much quicker than we can *feel* ourselves into a new way of acting. Worship is an *act* that develops feelings for God.

Think about the relationships that are most important to you—parents, spouse, siblings, children, close friends. What would happen if you paid attention to these loved ones only when you felt like it?

Describe a time when you had to resist your own feelings (tiredness, apathy, fear) in order to love well.

Writing to God

Thrones for righteous judgment
are set there, famous David-thrones.

Worship centers our attention on the decisions of God. The biblical word *judgment* means "the decisive word by which God straightens things out and puts things right." Thrones of judgment are the places that word is announced. Every time we worship our minds are informed, our memories refreshed with the judgments of God, we are familiarized with what God says, what he has decided, the ways he is working out our salvation.

We want to hear what God says and what he says to us: worship is the place where our attention is centered on these personal and decisive words of God.

What judgment of God—or word of God—has recently come home to you during worship? If it came through a song or a Scripture, write out the words. Revel in the way God "puts things right" in your life, among his people, in the world.

Pondering the Word

Pray for Jerusalem's peace!
  Prosperity to all you Jerusalem-lovers!
Friendly insiders, get along!
  Hostile outsiders, keep your distance!
For the sake of my family and friends,
  I say it again: live in peace!
For the sake of the house of our God, GOD,
  I'll do my very best for you.

In worship our basic needs suddenly become worthy of the dignity of creatures made in the image of God: peace and security. *Shalom,* peace, gathers all aspects of wholeness that result from God's will being completed in us. And *shalvah,* prosperity, connotes the relaxed stance of one who knows that everything is all right because God is over us, with us and for us in Jesus Christ.

In his quest for Jerusalem's peace and prosperity, what actions does the psalmist urge on others?

What is his own commitment?

How do prayer and human action come together in worship?

Worshiping God

Pray peace and prosperity for your community—family, friends, church, school, workplace. Use your imagination, guided by the Spirit. How might God's *shalom* and *shalvah* transform the lives of those you love, the corporate life of your community?

Worship initiates an extended, daily participation in peace and prosperity so that we share in our daily routines what God initiates and continues in Jesus Christ.

Thank God that your daily existence is a pilgrimage, that you are invited to journey into the rich life of the Trinity.

Worship does not satisfy our hunger for God—
it whets our appetite.
Our need for God overflows the hour
and permeates the week.

Five

SERVICE

*"Like Servants . . .
We're Watching & Waiting"
Psalm 123*

 Beginning to Obey ────────────────
I look to you, heaven-dwelling God,
   look up to you for help.

We are not presented with a functional god who will help us out
of jams or an entertainment god who will lighten tedious hours.
We are presented with the God of exodus and Easter, the God
of Sinai and Calvary. We would very soon become contemptu-
ous of a god whom we could figure out like a puzzle or learn to
use like a tool.

The moment we look up to God (and not over at him or
down on him) we are in the posture of servitude.

────────────────────────────────────

When have you been tempted to try to use God as a tool?

What does it mean to look *up* to God?

Worshiping God ─────────────────

Like servants, alert to their master's commands,
   like a maiden attending her lady,
We're watching and waiting, holding our breath,
   awaiting your word of mercy.
Mercy, GOD, mercy!

We live under the mercy. God does not treat us as alien others,
lining us up so that he can evaluate our competence or our use-
fulness or our worth. He rules, guides, commands, loves us as
children whose destinies he carries in his heart.

Praise God for his mercy; wait upon God's mercy. Fill this page
with your prayer.

Recording Your Journey

Mercy, GOD, mercy!
  We've been kicked around long enough,
Kicked in the teeth by complacent rich men,
  kicked when we're down by arrogant brutes.

The psalm is part of a vast literature of outcry, a longing for deliverance from oppression. The Christian realizes that every relationship that excludes God becomes oppressive. Recognizing and realizing that, we urgently want to live under the mastery of God.

What addictions are you, or have you been, especially prone to (alcohol, other substances, food, sex, shopping, games, gambling, lying, relationships)?

What pain, desire or need underlays the addictive behavior? If you have not previously considered this question, you may need to spend considerable time here, praying it through and asking God for wisdom.

How has "the mastery of God" set you free?

Pondering the Word

The best New Testament commentary on this psalm is in the final section of Paul's letter to the Romans: "So here's what I want you to do, God helping you: Take your everyday, ordinary life—your sleeping, eating, going-to-work, and walking-around life—and place it before God as an offering [*latreia*]" (12:1). The word *latreia* means "service," the work one does on behalf of the community. But it also is the base of our word *liturgy*, the service of worship that we render to God. We learn a relationship—an attitude toward life, a stance—of servitude before God, and then we are available to be of use to others in acts of service.

Read Romans 12:9-17. Choose two of the many commands in this passage, and consider: how does your worship of God enable you to serve others in these ways?

Writing to God

God's people are everywhere and always encouraged to work for the liberation of others, helping to free them from every form of bondage—religious, economic, cultural, political—that sin uses to stunt or thwart or cramp their lives.

Where do you feel called to "work for the liberation of others" —unborn children, refugees, the disabled, the poor, those who have never met Christ? Bring the need to God, asking for wisdom and strength. Ask God to give you his own heart for this person or group of people.

I have never yet heard a servant Christian complain of the oppressiveness of his servitude. I have never yet heard a servant Christian rail against the restrictions of her service. A servant Christian is the freest person on earth.

Write a prayer offering yourself more fully to God's service.

Six

HELP

"Oh, Blessed Be GOD!
He Didn't Go Off & Leave Us"
Psalm 124

Pondering the Word ————————————

If GOD hadn't been for us
  —all together now, Israel, sing out!—
If GOD hadn't been for us
  when everyone went against us,
We would have been swallowed alive
  by their violent anger,
Swept away by the flood of rage,
  drowned in the torrent;
We would have lost our lives
  in the wild, raging water.

Psalm 124 does not argue God's help; it does not explain God's help; it is a testimony of God's help in the form of a song. No longer does it seem of the highest priority to ask, "Why did this happen to me? Why do I feel left in the lurch?" Instead we ask, "How does it happen that there are people who sing with such confidence, 'God's strong name is our help'?"

Whom do you know who would sing this song with utmost confidence? Sit down with one such person; ask them to describe their experience of God's deliverance, and make notes here.

Psalm 124 is a magnification of the items of life that are thought to be unpleasant, best kept under cover, best surrounded with silence lest they clutter our lives with unpleasantness: the dragon's mouth, the flood's torrent, the snare's entrapment; suffering, catastrophe, disaster.

Beginning to Obey ———————————

The reason many of us do not ardently believe in the gospel is that we have never given it a rigorous testing, thrown our hard questions at it, faced it with our most prickly doubts.

Write down the hardest questions and prickliest doubts that come to mind when you read this psalm—or when you are in the midst of temptation and trouble.

Recording Your Journey

Oh, blessed be GOD!
 He didn't go off and leave us,
He didn't abandon us defenseless,
 helpless as a rabbit in a pack of snarling dogs.
We've flown free from their fangs,
 free of their traps, free as a bird.
Their grip is broken;
 we're free as a bird in flight.

Every day I put faith on the line. I persist in making the center of my life a God whom no eye hath seen, nor ear heard, whose will no one can probe. That's a risk.

Every day I put hope on the line. I don't know one thing about the future. Still, despite my ignorance, I say that God will accomplish his will and I cheerfully persist in living in the hope that nothing will separate me from Christ's love.

Every day I put love on the line. There is nothing I am less good at than love. And yet I decide, every day, to set aside what I can do best and attempt what I do very clumsily—open myself to the frustrations and failures of loving, daring to believe that failing in love is better than succeeding in pride.

Look closely at the risks you take as a Christian. What hazards do you face?

How has God come to your aid?

All that is hazardous work;
I live on the edge of defeat all the time.
But hazards or no hazards,
the fundamental reality we live with is God
who is "for us . . . GOD's strong name is our help."

Writing to God

GOD's strong name is our help,
the same GOD who made heaven and earth.

Psalm 124 is an instance of a person who digs deeply into the trouble and finds there the presence of the God who is on our side. In the details of the conflict, in the minuteness of a personal history, the majestic greatness of God becomes revealed. Faith develops out of the most difficult aspects of our existence, not the easiest.

As an act of prayer, write an honest description of the greatest trouble you face now—physical suffering, estrangement from someone you love, financial burdens, discouragement.

Ask the Lord to show you how he is with you in this trouble as the God who is *on your side*. Take time to let him speak to you.

Worshiping God

We speak our words of praise in a world that is hell-
ish; we sing our songs of victory in a world where
things get messy; we live our joy among people who neither un-
derstand nor encourage us. But the content of our lives is God,
not humanity. We are traveling in the light, toward God who is
rich in mercy and strong to save. It is the help we experience,
not the hazards we risk, that shapes our days.

Write a prayer celebrating God's presence and help.

Seven

SECURITY

"GOD Encircles His People"
Psalm 125

Recording Your Journey ─────────────

Backslider was a basic word in the religious vocabulary I learned as I grew up. Backsliding was everywhere and always an ominous possibility. Warnings were frequent and the sad consequences on public display. The mood was anxious and worried. I was taught to take my spiritual temperature every day, or at least every week; if it was not exactly "normal," there was general panic. I got the feeling that backsliding was not something you *did,* it happened to you. It was an accident that intruded on the unwary or an attack that involved the undefended.

What has your religious training taught you to believe about "backsliding" or "losing your salvation"?

What feelings did this teaching stir in you?

Writing to God ————————————————————

Those who trust in GOD
    are like Zion Mountain:
Nothing can move it, a rock-solid mountain
    you can always depend on.
Mountains encircle Jerusalem,
    and GOD encircles his people—
    always has and always will.

The emphasis of Psalm 125 is not on the precariousness of the Christian life but on its solidity. Living as a Christian is not walking a tightrope without a safety net; it is sitting secure in a fortress.

Like the mountains around Jerusalem, God protects his people. The psalmist highlights the qualities of *solidity* and *encircling/surrounding*. Write your response to the following questions in the form of prayers.

We can't see or touch God—so how can we experience him as solid?

What does it mean to you that God encircles you, encircles all his people?

Pondering the Word ——————————
How does each of the following Scriptures enrich
your understanding of God as your fortress?

Psalm 46:1

Psalm 91:9-10

John 17:11, 15

Beginning to Obey —————————————

I am full of faith one day and empty with doubt the next. I wake up one morning full of vitality, rejoicing in the sun; the next day I am gray and dismal, faltering and moody. I can be moved by nearly anything: sadness, joy, success, failure.

Yet as in the history of Israel, God is steadfastly with me, in mercy and judgment, insistently gracious. And so I learn to live not by my feelings about God but by the facts of God. I refuse to believe my depressions; I choose to believe in God.

My security comes from who God is, not from how I feel. Discipleship is a decision to live by what I know about God, not by what I *feel* about him or myself or my neighbors.

———————————————————————————

Think back to a time when you suffered from depression or discouragement. What doubts did you have about God? List these doubts and fears in the left-hand column. On the right, write what you know to be true about God, giving Scripture references if you can.

Recording Your Journey
The fist of the wicked
    will never violate
What is due the righteous,
    provoking wrongful violence.

Another source of uncertainty is our pain and suffering. Pain comes to those we love, and we conclude that there is no justice. We have the precarious feeling of living under a Damoclean sword. When will the ax fall on me?

If the evil fist is permanent, if there is no hope for salvation, even the most faithful and devout person will break and respond in "wrongful violence." But God does not permit that to happen. Evil is always temporary. Nothing counter to God's justice has any eternity to it.

When has your suffering, or the suffering of someone you love, led you to doubt your security in God?

How has evil shown itself to be temporary in your life?

Writing to God ——————————————

Be good to your good people, GOD,
    to those whose hearts are right!
GOD will round up the backsliders,
    corral them with the incorrigibles.

We know of Hymenaeus and Alexander, who "made shipwreck of their faith" (see 1 Tim 1:19-20). And if it is possible to defect, how do I know that I won't—or even worse, that I haven't? How do I know that I have not already lost faith, especially during times when I am depressed or have one calamity after another piled on me?

It is not possible to drift unconsciously from faith to perdition. You may choose the crooked way. God will not keep you against your will. But it is not the kind of thing you fall into by chance or slip into by ignorance. Defection requires a deliberate, sustained and determined act of rejection.

Perhaps the fear of losing our faith comes down to a misunderstanding of *power.* Are you strong enough to save yourself? Is God strong enough to save you?

Are you strong enough to turn permanently against God—to say a final no to his relentless love? Is God strong enough to keep you?

We wander like lost sheep, true; but God is a faithful shepherd
who pursues us relentlessly. All the persons of faith I
know are sinners, doubters, uneven performers.
We are secure not because we are sure of ourselves
but because we trust that God is sure of us.

Worshiping God ────────────

When we read "Peace over Israel!" we know that we are secure. God is running the show. There is nothing more certain than that he will accomplish his salvation in our lives and perfect his will in our histories.

Write a prayer of security, using images of solidity, encircling protection, a fortress, a rope that holds you and will not break.

Eight

JOY

"We Laughed, We Sang"
Psalm 126

Beginning to Obey ————————————————————

The enormous entertainment industry in America is a sign of the depletion of joy in our culture. We pay someone to make jokes, tell stories, perform dramatic actions, sing songs. We buy the vitality of another's imagination to divert and enliven our own poor lives. Society is a bored, gluttonous king employing a court jester to divert it after an overindulgent meal. But that kind of joy never penetrates our lives, never changes our basic constitution. When we run out of money, the joy trickles away.

———————————————————————————————

Has there been a time (including recently or currently) that you immersed yourself heavily in commercial entertainment?

What was the effect?

Joy is characteristic of Christian pilgrimage. It is not what we have to acquire in order to experience life in Christ; it is what comes to us when we are walking in the way of faith and obedience. Joy is a product of abundance; it is the overflow of vitality. It is life working together harmoniously. It is exuberance.

Whom do you know who is joyful in the Christian way—living in God's abundance? How does their joy express itself?

Recording Your Journey

It seemed like a dream, too good to be true,
    when GOD returned Zion's exiles.
We laughed, we sang,
    we couldn't believe our good fortune.
We were the talk of the nations—
    "GOD was wonderful to them!"
GOD *was* wonderful to us;
    we are one happy people.

We nurture these memories of laughter, these shouts of joy. We fill our minds with the stories of God's acts. Joy has a history. Joy is the verified, repeated experience of those involved in what God is doing. Joy is nurtured by living in such a history, building on such a foundation.

Take time to review the memory of one of God's great acts— your own conversion or someone else's, a healing, an improbable reconciliation between onetime enemies. Write out the story's high points.

A common but futile strategy for achieving joy is trying to eliminate things that hurt: get rid of pain by numbing the nerve
ends, get rid of insecurity by eliminating risks, get rid of disappointment by depersonalizing your relationships.

When have you tried to eliminate pain, insecurity or disappointment in these ways? What happened?

Writing to God ————————————————

And now, GOD, do it again—
    bring rains to our drought-stricken lives
So those who planted their crops in despair
    will shout hurrahs at the harvest,
So those who went off with heavy hearts
    will come home laughing, with armloads of
        blessing.

The watercourses of the Negeb are a network of ditches cut into the soil by wind and rain erosion. For most of the year they are baked dry under the sun, but a sudden rain makes the desert ablaze with blossoms. Our lives are like that—drought-stricken—and then, suddenly, the long years of barren waiting are interrupted by God's invasion of grace.

Think about one of your desert times. Did difficult circumstances bring on the barrenness? Or was it a dark night of the soul—a time of spiritual dryness?

Tell God how you experienced his "invasion of grace"—or if you are still waiting for it, tell him about the waiting.

The hard work of sowing seed in what looks like perfectly empty earth has, as every farmer knows, a time of harvest. All suffering, all pain, all emptiness, all disappointment is seed: sow it in God and he will, finally, bring a crop of joy from it.

Meditate on this planting image, coupled with Jesus' words "Unless a grain of wheat is buried in the ground, dead to the world, it is never any more than a grain of wheat. But if it is buried, it sprouts and reproduces itself many times over" (Jn 12:24). How was this true in Jesus' own life and death?

How is it true in your life?

Worshiping God

Laughter is a result of living in the midst of God's great works. There is plenty of suffering on both sides, past and future. The joy comes because God knows how to wipe away tears, and, in his resurrection work, create the smile of new life. Joy is an overflow of spirits that comes from feeling good not about yourself but about God. We find that his ways are dependable, his promises sure.

Are you willing to receive God's gift of joy? Respond in prayer.

Nine

WORK

"If GOD Doesn't Build the House"
Psalm 127

Beginning to Obey

Work is a major component in most lives. It is unavoidable. It can be either good or bad, an area where our sin is magnified or where our faith matures. For it is the nature of sin to take good things and twist them, ever so slightly, so that they miss the target to which they were aimed, the target of God. One requirement of discipleship is to learn the ways sin skews our nature and submit what we learn to the continuing will of God, so that we are reshaped through the days of our obedience.

What comments do your friends and colleagues make about their work? Do most of them seem to find it a blessing or a bane?

What jobs have you held over the years? Include such things as household chores in childhood, homemaking and volunteer positions.

What have you liked best about these jobs? disliked?

If GOD doesn't build the house,
    the builders only build shacks.
If GOD doesn't guard the city,
    the night watchman might as well nap.
It's useless to rise early and go to bed late,
    and work your worried fingers to the bone.
Don't you know he enjoys
    giving rest to those he loves?

Western culture deifies human effort as such. The machine is the symbol of this way of life which attempts to control and manage. Machines become more important than the people who use them.

Eastern culture manifests a deep-rooted pessimism regarding human effort. Since all work is tainted with selfishness and pride, the solution is to withdraw from all activity into pure being. The symbol of such an attitude is the Buddha—an enormous fat person sitting cross-legged, looking at his own navel.

With the development of global capitalism, of course, the Western attitude is currently prevailing. Give examples from your current or former workplace.

Where does each of these worldviews lead?

Western

Eastern

Ask God to open your mind to the biblical way.

Pondering the Word

"In the beginning God created." He *did* something. He *made* something. He fashioned heaven and earth. The week of creation was a week of work.

We live in a universe and in a history where God is working. Before anything else, work is an activity of God. The work of God is defined and described in the pages of Scripture. We have models of creation, acts of redemption, examples of help and compassion, paradigms of comfort and salvation. One of the reasons that Christians read Scripture repeatedly and carefully is to find out just how God works in Jesus Christ so that we can work in the name of Jesus Christ.

From your knowledge of Scripture, list verbs describing God's work *(create, seek, redeem . . .)*. Try to fill the page.

Jesus answered them, "My Father is still working,
and I also am working." (Jn 5:17 NRSV)

Recording Your Journey

Don't you see that children are GOD's best gift?
    the fruit of the womb his generous legacy?
Like a warrior's fistful of arrows
    are the children of a vigorous youth.
Oh, how blessed are you parents,
    with your quivers full of children!
Your enemies don't stand a chance against you;
    you'll sweep them right off your doorstep.

People are at the center of Christian work. The character of our work is shaped not by accomplishments or possessions but in the birth of relationships: "children are GOD's best gift." Among those around us we develop sons and daughters, sisters and brothers even as our Lord did with us.

Consider good work you have done (again, it need not have been paid). What human relationships were involved?

Who would you call your spiritual parent(s)? How did they invest in you?

The Genesis 1 record of creation shows how pleased God was with all his creatures, not just human beings ("and God saw that it was good"). The Fall brought alienation between human beings and the rest of creation (Gen 3:17-19), yet Paul tells us that Christ's reconciling work extends to the whole creation (Rom 8:19-23; Col 1:15-20).

Where in your work have you experienced the alienation depicted in Genesis 3? Examples: soil erosion, pollution, loss of species habitat, people's general disconnection from nature.

Have you experienced any reconciliation with the rest of creation? Examples: organic gardening; prairie, wetland or forest restoration; care for injured pets or wildlife.

Writing to God ───────────────────────

Relentless, compulsive work habits which our society rewards and admires are seen by the psalmist as a sign of weak faith and assertive pride, as if God could not be trusted to accomplish his will, as if we could rearrange the universe by our own effort.

What do you need to confess in regard to your work? Bring it to the Lord—and then give thanks that your work is at the periphery and God's work is at the center.

Worshiping God

Go back to your list of God's "working" verbs ("Pondering the Word" section of this chapter). Write a prayer thanking God for specific ways he has carried out his work in your life and in the lives of those around you.

Ten

HAPPINESS

"Enjoy the Blessing! Revel in the Goodness!"
Psalm 128

 Beginning to Obey ─────────────────

All you who fear GOD, how blessed you are!
   how happily you walk on his smooth
      straight road!
You worked hard and deserve all you've
     got coming.
     Enjoy the blessing! Revel in the goodness!

The easiest thing in the world is to be a Christian. What is hard is to be a sinner. Being a Christian is what we were created for. The life of faith has the support of an entire creation and the resources of a magnificent redemption. The history we walk in has been repeatedly entered by God, most notably in Jesus Christ, first to show us and then to help us live full of faith and exuberant with purpose. In the course of Christian discipleship we discover that without Christ we were doing it the hard way and that with Christ we are doing it the easy way. *Blessing* is the word that describes this happy state of affairs.

Give examples of the blessings, the rewards, that you've found to be inherent in following Jesus.

Pondering the Word

You're blessed when you're at the end of your rope. With less of you there is more of God and his rule.

You're blessed when you feel you've lost what is most dear to you. Only then can you be embraced by the One most dear to you.

You're blessed when you're content with just who you are—no more, no less. That's the moment you find yourselves proud owners of everything that can't be bought.

You're blessed when you've worked up a good appetite for God. He's food and drink in the best meal you'll ever eat.

You're blessed when you care. At the moment of being "care-full," you find yourselves cared for.

You're blessed when you get your inside world—your mind and heart—put right. Then you can see God in the outside world.

You're blessed when you can show people how to cooperate instead of compete or fight. That's when you discover who you really are, and your place in God's family.

You're blessed when your commitment to God provokes persecution. The persecution drives you even deeper into God's kingdom.

Not only that—count yourselves blessed every time people put you down or throw you out or speak lies about you to discredit you. What it means is that the truth is too close for comfort and they are uncomfortable. You can be glad when that happens— give a cheer, even!—for though they don't like it, *I* do! And all heaven applauds. And know that you are in good company. My prophets and witnesses have always gotten into this kind of trouble. (Mt 5:3-12)

Jesus, in his introduction to his Sermon on the Mount, identifies the eight key qualities in the life of a person of faith and announces each one with the word *blessed*. He makes it clear that the way of discipleship is not a reduction of what we already are, not an attenuation of our lives, not a subtraction from what we are used to. Rather, he will expand our capacities and fill us up with life so that we overflow with joy.

Meditate slowly through these statements of blessedness. Whom do you know who best exemplifies each of them? How is God working them into your life? How has your life grown larger, your capacities expanded, as you have drawn closer to God?

Recording Your Journey ———————————
Your wife will bear children as a vine bears grapes,
   your household lush as a vineyard,
The children around your table
   as fresh and promising as young olive shoots.

The illustration is, as we would expect, conditioned by Hebrew culture, in which the standard signs of happiness were a wife who had many children and children who gathered and grew around the table. But the meaning is still with us: Blessing has inherent in it the power to increase. It functions by sharing and delight in life.

Take time to trace generations of blessing in your physical or spiritual lineage. Who introduced you to Jesus? Who are that person's spiritual ancestors? How has the blessing spilled over from your life into the lives of your children (biological and spiritual) and thence into the lives of others? You may need to make some phone calls or write letters or e-mails to trace these stories—and you may end up with quite a complex, intricate family tree!

Life consists in the constant meeting of souls, which must share
their contents with each other. The blessed gives to the others,
because the strength instinctively pours from him and up
around him. . . . The characteristic of blessing is to multiply.
(*Johannes Pedersen*, Israel: Its Life and Culture)

Writing to God

Too much of the world's happiness depends on taking from one to satisfy another. To increase my standard of living, people in another part of the world must lower theirs. Industrialized nations acquire appetites for more and more luxuries and higher and higher standards of living, and increasing numbers of people are made poor and hungry. We have a greed problem: if I don't grab mine while I can, I might not be happy. The hunger problem is not going to be solved by government or by industry but in church, among Christians who learn a different way to pursue happiness.

In what ways have consumerism and greed made war on your soul?

What new habits of prayer and action could help you live in greater simplicity, contentment and blessedness? Ask God for wisdom.

Worshiping God

Stand in awe of God's Yes.
  Oh, how he blesses the one who fears GOD!

Enjoy the good life in Jerusalem
  every day of your life.
And enjoy your grandchildren.
  Peace to Israel!

We accept the announced and proclaimed truth that God is at the center of our existence, find out how he has constructed this world (his creation), how he has provided for our redemption, and proceed to walk in that way. The Bible isn't interested in whether we believe in God or not. It assumes that everyone more or less does. What it is interested in is the response we have to him: will we let God be as he is, majestic and holy, vast and wondrous, or will we always be trying to whittle him down to the size of our small minds?

Pray a prayer of blessedness, standing in awe of God's Yes.

Eleven

PERSEVERANCE

"They Never Could Keep Me Down"
Psalm 129

Pondering the Word————————————

"They've kicked me around ever since I was young"
—this is how Israel tells it—
"They've kicked me around ever since I was young,
 but they never could keep me down.
Their plowmen plowed long furrows
 up and down my back;
But GOD wouldn't put up with it,
 he sticks with us;
GOD ripped the harnesses
 of the evil plowmen to shreds."

Do you think of Christian faith as a fragile style of life that can flourish only when weather conditions are just right, or do you see it as a tough perennial that can stick it out through storm and drought, survive the trampling of careless feet and the attacks of vandals? The apostle Paul looks back over his own life and provides powerful support for the latter view:

I have been beaten times without number. I have faced death again and again. I have been beaten the regulation thirty-nine stripes by the Jews five times. I have been beaten with rods three times. I have been stoned once. I have been shipwrecked three times. I have been twenty-four hours in the open sea. In my travels I have been in constant danger from rivers, from bandits, from my own countrymen, and from pagans. I have faced danger on the high seas, danger among false Christians. I have known drudgery, exhaustion, many sleepless nights, hunger and thirst, fasting, cold and exposure. Apart from all external trials I have the daily burden of responsibility for all the churches. Do you think anyone is weak without my feeling his weakness? Does anyone have his faith upset without my burning indignation? (2 Cor 11:23-29 Phillips)

Despite all this, at the end of his life, among the last words he wrote is this sentence: "I've got my eye on the goal, where God is beckoning us onward—to Jesus. I'm off and running, and I'm not turning back" (Phil 3:13-14).

In the 2 Corinthians passage, how does Paul emphasize the frequency or constancy of his struggles?

Does he find the struggle worth it? What attitude does the Philippians passage express?

Make a list of Christians you know whose faith has endured through hardship and suffering. Thank God for each of them.

Recording Your Journey —————————

Oh, let all those who hate Zion
     grovel in humiliation;
Let them be like grass in shallow ground
     that withers before the harvest,
Before the farmhands can gather it in,
     the harvesters get in the crop,
Before the neighbors have a chance to call out,
     "Congratulations on your wonderful crop!
     We bless you in GOD's name!"

The way of the world is peppered with brief enthusiasms, like the grass on that half-inch of topsoil, springing up so wonderfully and without effort, but as quickly withering. The way of the world is marked by proud, God-defying purposes, unharnessed from eternity and therefore worthless and futile.

Choose one of the psalm's images of futility—trying to plow up Israel's back with a disconnected harness, or trying to harvest grain from shallow soil—and relate it to a situation you have encountered. How have you seen God frustrate the purposes of those who oppose him?

Writing to God

It is apathetic, sluggish neutrality that is death to perseverance, acts like a virus in the bloodstream and enervates the muscles of discipleship. The person who makes excuses for hypocrites and rationalizes the excesses of the wicked, who loses a sense of opposition to sin, who obscures the difference between faith and denial, grace and selfishness—*that* is the person to be wary of.

"Whatever." It's a common response these days, accompanied by a shrug. We are often afraid of passion and risk—yet fear is not God's way. Wherever you have tried to protect yourself, to hide behind apathy, open your life to God. Record your thoughts and experiences here.

It is regarding the things we care about that we are capable of expressing anger. The way of faith centers and absorbs our lives, and when someone makes the way difficult, throws stumbling blocks in the path of the innocent, creates difficulties for those young in faith and unpracticed in obedience, there is anger: "Oh, let all those who hate Zion grovel in humiliation!" We offer up our anger to God, who trains us in creative love.

Some, conditioned to "be nice," haven't learned how to tap into the positive energy of anger. Others are all too ready to fly off the handle; their anger destroys them and others. Which is your tendency?

Offer your anger to God, asking him to channel it through courage and self-control.

Beginning to Obey

The central reality for Christians is the personal, unalterable, persevering commitment God makes to us. Perseverance is not the result of *our* determination, it is the result of God's faithfulness. We survive in the way of faith not because we have extraordinary stamina but because God is righteous, because God sticks with us.

God sticks with us. Take ten minutes to be silent, allowing this statement to reverberate in your mind and heart. Write down any thoughts and questions that come to the surface.

Where is your greatest need to persevere? How is God challenging you to trust him and lean on him in this area? Write down any actions you feel called to take.

Worshiping God

Strip down, start running—and never quit! No extra spiritual fat, no parasitic sins. Keep your eyes on *Jesus,* who both began and finished this race we're in. Study how he did it. Because he never lost sight of where he was headed—that exhilarating finish in and with God—he could put up with anything along the way: cross, shame, whatever. And now he's *there,* in the place of honor, right alongside God. In this all-out match against sin, others have suffered far worse than you, to say nothing of what Jesus went through—all that bloodshed! (Heb 12:1-3)

Pray with your eyes on Jesus. Express thanks for his willingness to persevere through suffering for your sake.

Twelve

HOPE

*"I Pray to GOD . . . and
Wait for What He'll Say & Do"
Psalm 130*

Beginning to Obey ─────────────
To be human is to be in trouble. And a Christian is a
person who decides to face and live through suffering. If we do not make that decision, we are endangered on every side. A man or woman of faith who fails to acknowledge and deal with suffering becomes, at last, either a cynic or a melancholic or a suicide.

───────────────────────────

Our society offers many ways to try to avoid our suffering. List as many as you can.

Which are most tempting to you, and why?

There is an American myth that denies suffering
and the sense of pain. It acts as if they *should* not be,
and hence it devalues the *experience* of suffering.
But this myth denies our encounter with reality. *(Ivan Illich)*

Pondering the Word

Help, GOD—the bottom has fallen out of my life!
  Master, hear my cry for help!
Listen hard! Open your ears!
  Listen to my cries for mercy.

By setting the anguish out in the open and voicing it as a prayer, the psalm gives dignity to our suffering. In suffering we enter *the depths;* we are at the heart of things; we are near to where Christ was on the cross.

What does it mean to suffer well? Give examples from Jesus' last days. Consider how he entered fully into suffering, without denial and without self-pity.

Recording Your Journey

Many people suffer because of the false supposition on which they have based their lives. That supposition is that there should be no fear or loneliness, no confusion or doubt. But these sufferings can only be dealt with creatively when they are understood as wounds integral to our human condition. Therefore ministry is a very *confronting* service. It does not allow people to live with illusions of immortality and wholeness. It keeps reminding others that they are mortal and broken, but also that with the recognition of this condition, liberation starts.
(Henri Nouwen)

The Son of God suffered unto the death, not that men might not suffer, but that their sufferings might be like His.
(George MacDonald)

Reflect on the quotes above. How can facing our suffering be liberating?

How have you found it so?

Writing to God ——————————————

If you, GOD, kept records on wrongdoings,
   who would stand a chance?
As it turns out, forgiveness is your habit,
   and that's why you're worshiped.

Psalm 130 immerses the suffering in God. "God's very being is mercy. The mercy of God lies in His readiness to share in sympathy the distress of another, a readiness which springs from His inmost nature and stamps all His being and doing" (Karl Barth). This is why we know that suffering can never be ultimate, it can never constitute the bottom line. God is at the foundation and God is at the boundaries. If God were different than he is, not one of us would have a leg to stand on.

If you are currently suffering, or if you have been praying for someone who is suffering deeply, ask God to reveal his presence in the midst of the suffering. Like the psalmist, picture yourself in a dark pit ("the depths"). Where is God?

You may want to leave the rest of this page blank; or use it to record God's revelation of his presence.

I pray to GOD—my life a prayer—
  and wait for what he'll say and do.
My life's on the line before God, my Lord,
    waiting and watching till morning,
    waiting and watching till morning.

Wait and *watch* are at the center of the psalm. *Wait* and *watch* add up to *hope*. The Christian's waiting and watching—that is, hoping—is based on the conviction that God is actively involved in his creation and vigorously at work in redemption.

Hoping means going about our assigned tasks, confident that God will provide the meaning and the conclusions. It means a confident, alert expectation that God will do what he said he will do. It is imagination put in the harness of faith.

Write out some of God's promises, things he has said he will do on behalf of those he loves. Use Scripture, perhaps including texts you've explored in earlier pages of this journal. Ask God to help you *swallow* these truths—absorb them and make them part of you.

Despair all too readily embraces the ills it foresees;
hope is an energy and arouses the mind to explore every
possibility to combat them. *(Thornton Wilder)*

Worshiping God

Oh Israel, wait and watch for GOD—
with GOD's arrival comes love,
with GOD's arrival comes generous redemption.
No doubt about it—he'll redeem Israel,
buy back Israel from captivity to sin.

The big difference is not in what people suffer but in the way they suffer. The psalm does not exhort us to put up with suffering; it does not explain it or explain it away. It is, rather, a powerful demonstration that our place in the depths is not out of bounds from God.

Thank God for his generous mercy, and for hope that is real.

Thirteen

HUMILITY

"I've Kept My Feet on the Ground"
Psalm 131

 Beginning to Obey ─────────────
Pruning is an annual practice among people who care about growing things. It always looks like an act of mutilation. It appears that you are ruining the plant when, in fact, you are helping it.

Jesus said, "[The Father] cuts off every branch of me that doesn't bear grapes. And every branch that is grape-bearing he prunes back so that it will bear even more" (Jn 15:2).

Pray, opening your heart to the pruning work that God may want to do today.

> GOD, I'm not trying to rule the roost,
>   I don't want to be king of the mountain.
> I haven't meddled where I have no business
>   or fantasized grandiose plans.
> I've kept my feet on the ground,
>   I've cultivated a quiet heart.

Our culture encourages and rewards ambition without qualification. We are surrounded by a way of life in which betterment is understood as expansion, as acquisition, as fame. We are caught up in a way of life that, instead of delighting in finding out the meaning of God and searching out the conditions in which human qualities can best be realized, recklessly seeks ways to circumvent nature, arrogantly defies personal relationships and names God only in curses.

List ways this overweening ambition is being played out in the culture. You may find examples in advertising slogans, technological developments, pop psychology and the personal choices of people you know.

How have you bought into some of these ideas?

Pondering the Word

I am the Real Vine and my Father is the Farmer. He cuts off every branch of me that doesn't bear grapes. And every branch that is grape-bearing he prunes back so it will bear even more. You are already pruned back by the message I have spoken.

Live in me. Make your home in me just as I do in you. In the same way that a branch can't bear grapes by itself but only by being joined to the vine, you can't bear fruit unless you are joined with me.

I am the Vine, you are the branches. When you're joined with me and I with you, the relation intimate and organic, the harvest is sure to be abundant. Separated, you can't produce a thing. Anyone who separates from me is deadwood, gathered up and thrown on the bonfire. But if you make yourselves at home with me and my words are at home in you, you can be sure that whatever you ask will be listened to and acted upon. This is how my Father shows who he is—when you produce grapes, when you mature as my disciples. (Jn 15:1-8)

How does Jesus combine imagery of a fruit-bearing vine with images of being at home ("abiding" in older translations)?

How does the picture of being part of Jesus' vine challenge your notions of self-sufficiency?

What does it mean to depend on God without infantile dependency? (How does the imagery of the vine help answer this question?)

What are the consequences of being cut off from the vine?

Do you experience your relationship with Jesus as *living with* him, making your home with him? How would you like that "at-home" experience to grow?

Recording Your Journey ————————————
It is difficult to recognize unruly ambition as a sin
because it has a kind of superficial relationship to
the virtue of aspiration—an impatience with mediocrity and a
dissatisfaction with all things created until we are at home with
the Creator, the hopeful striving for the best God has for us.
Ambition is aspiration gone crazy. Aspiration is the channeled,
creative energy that moves us to growth in Christ, shaping goals
in the Spirit. Ambition takes these same energies for growth and
development and uses them to make something tawdry and
cheap.

Is your tendency to fall into prideful ambition or to avoid setting goals and remain content with mediocrity? Where has this
set you back in your life with God?

In either case, take time to speak this prayer to God:

> I will not try to run my own life or the lives of others; that is
> God's business. I will not pretend to invent the meaning of the
> universe; I will accept what God has shown its meaning to be. I
> will not strut about demanding that I be treated as the center of
> my family or my neighborhood or my work, but seek to discover
> where I fit and do what I am good at.

Writing to God ———————————————

Like a baby content in its mother's arms,
  my soul is a baby content.

The Christian is

not like an infant crying loudly for his mother's breast, but like a
weaned child that quietly rests by his mother's side, happy in
being with her. . . . No desire now comes between him and his
God; for he is sure that God knows what he needs before he asks
him. And just as the child gradually breaks off the habit of
regarding his mother only as a means of satisfying his own desires
and learns to love her for her own sake, so the worshipper after a
struggle has reached an attitude of mind in which he desires God
for himself and not as a means of fulfillment of his own wishes.
His life's centre of gravity has shifted. He now rests no longer in
himself but in God. *(Arthur Weiser)*

It is no easy thing to quiet yourself: sooner may we calm the sea
or rule the wind or tame a tiger than quiet ourselves. It is
pitched battle. Many who have traveled this way of faith have
described the transition from an infantile faith that grabs at God
out of desperation to a mature faith that responds to God out of
love.

How has God been weaning you? In what ways is he calling you
to grow up?

Worshiping God

Wait, Israel, for GOD. Wait with hope.
Hope now; hope always!

We need pruning. Cut back to our roots, we learn this psalm and discover the quietness of the weaned child, the tranquillity of maturing trust.

Spend time in silence with God—asking for nothing, just being alert to his presence. He knows your needs, and you know that he is faithful and full of mercy.

Fourteen

OBEDIENCE

"How He Promised GOD"
Psalm 132

Beginning to Obey ——————————————

The most religious places in the world, as a matter of fact, are not churches but battlefields and mental hospitals. You are much more likely to find passionate prayer in a foxhole than in a church pew; and you will certainly find more otherworldly visions and supernatural voices in a mental hospital than you will in a church.

Nevertheless we Christians don't go to either place to nurture our faith. We want a Christian faith that has stability but is not petrified, that has vision but is not hallucinatory. How do we get the adult maturity to keep our feet on the ground and retain the childlike innocence to make the leap of faith?

Have you ever experienced—or witnessed—"foxhole religion"?

Do you know anyone, young or old, who exhibits a healthy maturity alongside a childlike freedom? Give examples of how these qualities are played out.

Recording Your Journey ————————————

O GOD, remember David,
  remember all his troubles!
And remember how he promised GOD,
  made a vow to the Strong God of Jacob,
"I'm not going home,
  and I'm not going to bed,
I'm not going to sleep,
  not even take time to rest,
Until I find a home for GOD,
  a house for the Strong God of Jacob."
Remember how we got the news in Ephrathah,
  learned all about it at Jaar Meadows?
We shouted, "Let's go to the shrine dedication!
  Let's worship at God's own footstool!"
Up, GOD, enjoy your new place of quiet repose,
  you and your mighty covenant ark;
Get your priests all dressed up in justice;
  prompt your worshipers to sing this prayer:
"Honor your servant David;
  don't disdain your anointed one."

The ark of the covenant, a symbol of God's presence, had accompanied Israel from Sinai, through the wilderness wanderings, had been captured by the enemy Philistines and was returned to Israel, to the village of Kiriath-jearim. News had come to David of where the ark was; he vowed to get it and was obedient to his vow. He brought it up to Jerusalem in festive parade.

There is a vast, rich reality of obedience beneath the feet of disciples. They are not the first persons to ascend these slopes on their way of obedience to God, and they will not be the last. This history is important, for without it we are at the mercy of whims. Memory is a databank we use to evaluate our position and make decisions. With a biblical memory, we have two thousand years of experience from which to make the off-the-cuff responses that are required each day in the life of faith.

We need the community of experience of brothers and sisters in the church, the centuries of experience provided by our biblical ancestors. A Christian who has David in his bones, Jeremiah in his bloodstream, Paul in his fingertips and Christ in his heart will know how much and how little value to put on his own momentary feelings and the experience of the past week.

The Israelites were instructed to saturate their lives with God's word, God's commandments (see Deut 6:6-8). Would you describe yourself as well saturated in the stories and teachings of Scripture?

List the various ways you encounter Scripture (quiet time, memorization, congregational reading, small group Bible study, praise songs, recordings).

How can you give the Bible a larger place in your day-to-day life?

When have biblical knowledge and the hard-won wisdom of believing friends helped you make good choices—both in day-to-day life and at major turning points? Be as specific as possible.

Pondering the Word

GOD gave David his word,
   he won't back out on this promise:
"One of your sons
   I will set on your throne;
If your sons stay true to my Covenant
   and learn to live the way I teach them,
Their sons will continue the line—
   always a son to sit on your throne.
Yes—I, GOD, chose Zion,
   the place I wanted for my shrine;
This will always be my home;
   this is what I want, and I'm here for good.
I'll shower blessings on the pilgrims who come here,
   and give supper to those who arrive hungry;
I'll dress my priests in salvation clothes;
   the holy people will sing their hearts out!
Oh, I'll make the place radiant for David!
   I'll fill it with light for my anointed!
I'll dress his enemies in dirty rags,
   but I'll make his crown sparkle with splendor."

Obedience is not a stodgy plodding in the ruts of religion, it is a hopeful race toward God's promises.

Think about God's promises cited in Psalm 132. How do they echo God's work recorded in Scripture? Which has particular resonance for you, and why?

I'll shower blessings on the pilgrims who come here, and give supper to those who arrive hungry.

I'll dress my priests in salvation clothes; the holy people will sing their hearts out!

Oh, I'll make the place radiant for David! I'll fill it with light for my anointed!

I'll dress his enemies in dirty rags, but I'll make his crown sparkle with splendor.

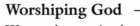 **Worshiping God**

We need roots in the past to give obedience ballast and breadth; we need a vision of the future to give obedience direction and goal. Obedience is the strength to stand and the willingness to leap, and the sense to know when to do which. Which is exactly what we get when an accurate memory of God's ways is combined with a lively hope in his promises.

Pray to grow in the grace of obedience. Make any necessary commitments to increase your familiarity with Scripture so you can gain a deeper knowledge of God's ways.

Fifteen

COMMUNITY

"Like Costly Anointing Oil
Flowing Down Head & Beard"
Psalm 133

Recording Your Journey ————————————
We can no more be a Christian and have nothing to
do with the church than we can be a person and not
be in a family. Membership in the church is a basic spiritual fact
for those who confess Christ as Lord. It is part of the fabric of
redemption. God never makes private, secret salvation deals
with people. His relationships with us are personal, true; intimate, yes; but private, no. We are a family in Christ. No Christian is an only child.

So the question is not "Am I going to be a part of a community of faith?" but "How am I going to live in this community of
faith?"

___

How have you so far chosen to relate to God's people—your
family of faith?

☐ avoid it/run away

☐ make occasional visits—especially on Christmas and Easter

☐ stay involved but criticize everything

☐ learn how to function in it harmoniously and joyously

Beginning to Obey

How wonderful, how beautiful,
   when brothers and sisters get along!

Creation itself was not complete until there was community, Adam needing Eve before humanity was whole. God never works with individuals in isolation, but always with people in community. Jesus worked with twelve disciples and lived with them in community. The church was formed when one hundred twenty people were "all together" in one place. The Bible knows nothing of a religion defined by what a person does inwardly in the privacy of thought or feeling, or apart from others on lonely retreat.

Do you find this understanding of God's ways puzzling, questionable or natural?

How does your cultural background play into your response? (Consider, for example, that North Americans tend to think individualistically, while people from Asian and African cultures highly prize community.)

Children are ordinarily so full of their own needs and wants that they look at a brother or sister not as an ally but as a competitor. And so if we are going to sing "How wonderful, how beautiful when brothers and sisters get along," we will not do it by being left to ourselves, following our natural bent.

It is far easier to deal with people as problems to be solved than to have anything to do with them in community. If a person can be isolated from the family and then be professionally counseled, advised and guided without the complications of all of those relationships, things are very much simpler. But if such practices are engaged in systematically, they become an avoidance of community.

Another common way to avoid community is to turn the church into an institution. Goals are set that will catch the imagination of the largest numbers of people; structures are developed that will accomplish the goal through planning and organization. In the process the church becomes less and less a community, that is, people who pay attention to each other ("brothers and sisters"), and more and more a collectivism of "contributing units."

Where have you seen these distortions of community? What was the effect?

Writing to God ————————————————————

It's like costly anointing oil
  flowing down head and beard,
Flowing down Aaron's beard,
  flowing down the collar of his priestly robes.

The oil is an anointing oil, marking the person as a priest. My brother, my sister, is my priest. When we see the other as God's anointed, our relationships are profoundly affected.

What Christ has done is anoint us with his Spirit. We are set apart for service to one another. We mediate to one another the mysteries of God. We represent to one another the address of God. We are priests who speak God's Word and share Christ's sacrifice.

———————————————————————————————————

How would it change your experience of community if you consciously regarded your brothers and sisters as priests?

Begin now! List some of the people you worship with and make notes on how they are or could be priests to you—bringing God's words, mediating God's presence. Include at least one name of a person you find it hard to like. What might God want you to receive from them?

Pondering the Word ─────────────

It's like the dew on Mount Hermon
   flowing down the slopes of Zion.
Yes, that's where GOD commands the blessing,
   ordains eternal life.

Think about the scrub-desert setting in which the psalmist
wrote these words. What might dew have represented for him
and for the people of Israel who sang this song?

What verbs here describe God's action? How do they communi-
cate sureness?

Why do you think the concept of eternal life is introduced in
this celebration of the faith community? What does eternal life
have to do with our life together?

Recording Your Journey —————————

Important in any community of faith is an ever-renewed expectation in what God is doing with our brothers and sisters in the faith. We refuse to label the others as one thing or another. We refuse to predict our brother's behavior, our sister's growth.

A community of faith flourishes when we view each other with this expectancy, wondering what God will do today in this one, in that one. When we are in a community with those Christ loves and redeems, we are constantly finding out new things about them. They are new persons each morning, endless in their possibilities. We explore the fascinating depths of their friendship, share the secrets of their quest. It is impossible to be bored in such a community, impossible to feel alienated among such people.

Is it easy for you to label and categorize people? Give examples of your mental categories.

When have someone's words or actions broken your stereotypes and filled you with wonder?

Worshiping God ————————————————————
Pray for the grace of loving curiosity, a genuine openness to your brothers and sisters and eagerness to see God's work in their lives. If you are involved in conflict with other members of the Christian community, ask for creativity and courage to find a healthy resolution. Thank God for the gifts you have received through God's people.

Sixteen

BLESSING

"Lift Your Praising Hands"
Psalm 134

Beginning to Obey ─────────────────────────
While there are certainly difficulties in the way of
faith, it cannot by any stretch of the imagination be
called dull. It requires everything that is in us; it enlists all our
desires and abilities; it gathers our total existence into its songs.
But when we get to where we are going, what then? What happens at the end of faith? What takes place when we finally arrive?
Will we be disappointed?

───

What are some of your mental pictures of "the end of faith," the
final arrival?

Do any of them betray a fear of disappointment?

Where does your imagination need to grow so that you can be
open to God's promise of blessing?

Pondering the Word

Come, bless GOD,
    all you servants of GOD!
You priests of GOD, posted to the nightwatch
    in GOD's shrine,
Lift your praising hands to the Holy Place,
    and bless GOD.
In turn, may GOD of Zion bless you—
    GOD who made heaven and earth!

God gets down on his knees among us, gets on our level and shares himself with us. He does not reside afar off and send us diplomatic messages; he kneels among us. That posture is characteristic of God. God enters into our need, he anticipates our goals, he "gets into our skin" and understands us better than we do ourselves. That is *blessing*.

And because God blesses us, we bless God. We participate in the process that God has initiated and continues. We who are blessed, bless. When the word is used for what people do, it has, in Scripture, the sense of "praise and gratitude for blessing received" *(Interpreter's Dictionary)*. The people who learn what it is like to receive the blessing, persons who travel the way of faith experiencing the ways of grace in all kinds of weather and over every kind of terrain, become good at blessing.

In the psalm, how are those who bless God described?

How is God described?

Do you know "what it is like to receive the blessing"? Are you becoming "good at blessing"?

Recording Your Journey ─────────

We are invited to bless the Lord; we are commanded to bless the Lord. And then someone says, "But I don't feel like it. And I won't be a hypocrite. I can't bless God if I don't feel like blessing God. It wouldn't be honest."

The biblical response to that is "Lift up your praising hands to the Holy Place, and bless GOD!" You can lift up your hands regardless of how you feel; it is a simple motor movement. You may not be able to command your heart, but you can command your arms. We are psychosomatic beings; body and spirit are intricately interrelated. Go through the motions of blessing God and your spirit will pick up the cue and follow along.

Do your feelings often block you from blessing and worshiping God?

How have you experienced the link between "going through the motions" and beginning to "feel like it"? Think of times you have worked on building a new habit, or acquired a taste for a food you initially found strange.

The main thing is not work for the Lord; it is not suffering in the name of the Lord; it is not witnessing to the Lord; it is not teaching Sunday school for the Lord; it is not being responsible for the sake of the Lord in the community; it is not keeping the Ten Commandments; not loving your neighbor; not observing the golden rule. "The chief end of man is to glorify God and enjoy him forever." Or, in the vocabulary of Psalm 134, "Bless GOD."

All the movements of discipleship arrive at a place where joy is experienced. Every step of assent toward God develops the capacity to enjoy. Not only is there, increasingly, more to be enjoyed, there is steadily the acquired ability to enjoy it.

What priorities for Christian living have been emphasized in your discipleship so far? Examples: witnessing, church work, quiet time or devotions, service.

Does "learning to enjoy God" have a place on your list? If so, how did it get there? If not, why does enjoying God seem strange or unimportant?

Writing to God

The great Swiss theologian Karl Barth never took himself seriously and always took God seriously, and therefore he was full of cheerfulness, exuberant with blessing. Always and everywhere we are aware that Barth was responding to God's grace; there is a chuckle rumbling underneath his most serious prose; there is a twinkle on the edges of his eyes—always.

Tell God about the situations in which you would like to take yourself less seriously and take him more seriously.

Have you cultivated the habit of gratitude? Fill this page with thanksgivings—acknowledgments of God's blessings.

Worshiping God ————————————

All the way to heaven is heaven. *(Catherine of Siena)*

On your journey of faith how have you been learning to be a disciple and a pilgrim instead of a tourist?

What have you been learning about God? Write your answer as a prayer.